MAN, GREED,
AND THE ECONOMY

MAN, GREED,
AND THE ECONOMY

Joseph Lacerenza

Library of Congress Control Number:		2011910419
ISBN:	Hardcover	978-1-4628-9350-8
	Softcover	978-1-4628-9351-5
	Ebook	978-1-4628-9352-2

To order additional copies of this book, contact:
Xlibris Corporation
1-888-795-4274
www.Xlibris.com
Orders@Xlibris.com
101205

CONTENTS

INTRODUCTION

I'm writing this book mainly for intellectuals; though it's coarse and trades politeness for candor, those with instinct will see beyond what I'm saying, also, as an unusual challenging perspective on our current state of affairs. It's a condensed study of man and some of those things that has shaped his existence, so the story will start from the beginnings of man encompassing some of those things I see to be contributing factors in his development. So unless you want to know what I believe to be the truth, you should not read this book .Since religion is a factor in the Middle East There will be religion in the scientific sense of the word, which does evolve, since money is a factor We will look at money and certainly greed as a trait of man and where we are going because of it; so be prepared for the strangest read you have ever encountered. This book may make you mad enough to put it down, but I urge you once you start reading it—even if you have to put it down in anger—please pick it back up once you've cooled off and finish it. You paid for it; you might as well get your money's worth.

CHAPTER 1

Since the Bible is the most published book in history, I started there. Unfortunately, it says very little about Adam and Eve. At the end of the Bible, it warns those that add or detract from the Bible will be cursed, which is a frightening thought; but I thought, *What harm is there in research?* So I read the *Vita*, which was left out of the Bible (the life of Adam and Eve). In reading it, I realized there were reasons why it was left out, but everything fitted together like a puzzle, which is why I'm including it here. But I would say, if you choose to read it, you should remember why it was left out of the Bible. The reasons will be obvious to you as you read it.

Money first appears in the Bible in Genesis where it speaks of gold being in the Garden of Eden and that God put it there possibly as a temptation. Odd how if you add one letter to G*od*, it becomes *gold*, and both are worshipped. But we must choose one and forsake the other. Is this where greed begins? God told Moses in describing himself (I am That I am), and again, when he fought with the Egyptians, Moses described God as the Lord of Hosts. So I think God is of mind and spirit and encompasses all the order of the universe and rules over it. Gold, on the other hand, is a metal, cold and dead, which got me to thinking Lead didn't start out as Lead. Lead started out as radium, which is hot and radioactive. As radium, it cooled off; it became denser, forming Lead. You can use gold to shield yourself from radiation. It is as dense as lead, so did gold start out as something radioactive? Did God use the radioactive version of gold to create a universe billions of years before he created this universe?

The *Vita* speaks about gold and the artificial light it gave to Adam and Eve in the Cave of Treasures. The Cave of Treasures was a place that God gave Adam and Eve to be their new home after he cast them out of the Garden of Eden. The premise is that God gave them the true light and security of his presence; and gold gives off artificial light and false security, yet in hard times, some of us run to gold and not to God.

Back to Adam and Eve. It seems that Adam and Eve were very unhappy being outside the Garden of Eden and prayed and pleaded with God continually for him to put them back into Eden, but God would not relent. He informed Adam that it would be 5,700 years before Adam and Eve would be allowed back into Eden, at Christ's crucifixion. You have to ask yourself, 5,700 years—that's a long time; how long did they live? Well, the Bible says that Adam lived 930 years, and Eve's age is unknown. It is stated in the Bible that when Adam died, Eve pounded her breasts and asked God to take her, and her body gave up its spirit. Nine hundred thirty years for Adam seems impossible. I started thinking he must have been ninety-three, but the Bible seems to be insistent, so more research brought me to another book that was left out of the Bible called the *Book of Enoch*. So I thought, *Let's look at this book and try and figure why it was left out of the Bible so I could make some sense of whether the information is valid enough to be used in my research*. My conclusions are that the *Vita* was left out for multiple reasons: First that Adam and Eve committed suicide and sacrificed their blood to God. This is important because God accepted blood sacrifice which evolved into burnt offerings, but he wanted animal sacrifice and not human sacrifice, which shows up in the Bible. Second, in the New Testament, God wanted husbands and wives to kneel together side by side in prayer (What so ever two people ask for in my sons name it shall be given). Adam asked Eve to go downstream to pray out of sight of him. God seems to like some forms of sacrifice Adam made and didn't like others, so he commanded Abraham to make certain forms of sacrifice that he found pleasing.

God's relationship with Abraham must have been one of absolute faithfulness on Abraham's part. I thought about it. Abraham had Sarah; she was beautiful. His love for her was absolute even when she told him to go to her maidservant to have children. He gave in, but shouldn't have. He had children with concubines. His firstborn, Ishmael, who would have normally received the birthright, was pushed away for Isaac, the child from the woman that Abraham loved—Sarah. It's important because Abraham's willingness to sacrifice Isaac, the child he loved best because he came from the love of his life, Sarah, is why God would be willing to sacrifice his only son; but this is also what has bred the hostilities between Jews and Arabs. This all seems like we are talking religion, but bear with me; it comes together as a puzzle.

Let's go back to Enoch, who lived 365 years, and God took him 365 years; 930 years for Adam. The *Book of Enoch* tells how time is kept, and it is how we keep time today. If this is true, then Adam actually lived 930 of our years. How's this possible? Where is there proof of this? Well, first the *Book of Enoch* was left out of the Bible because people used the knowledge of timekeeping to do astrology, sorcery, and soothsaying, which God abhors; so it was left out of the Bible, but we do have another written translation of it, only it is in a language that is not in the Bible.

After Enoch's time, man wanted to put himself on the same level as God, so man started to build a tower to heaven. The Bible calls it the Tower of Babel. God got so angry that he confused the people who all used to speak one language. God put all different languages in their minds and scattered them to the four corners of the world. One of these people settled in South America; we call them the Mayans. They continued to build pyramids in the mountains and perverted animal sacrifices to human sacrifices, so God got angry and removed them. Their 2012 prediction was for the ending of the age, which puts us at the end of one age and the beginning of another age. How long the transfer will take is anyone's guess. The Bible says it's called the tribulation period, and it takes seven years, a time when the god of gold (greed, idols that represent the devil) fails and the God of heaven prevails.

There are so many other things going on while this is happening in our present day that we don't see the basics happening. In ancient days, you were doing really well by just staying alive, let alone maintaining a mistress and a penthouse; so life, I guess, has become too complicated to see where we are leading ourselves. Personally, when we went off the gold standard, I realized we were headed into trouble. My high school ring was $37 and was heavy. I no longer have it; I sold it when gold was $70 an ounce. Yeah, I got stung, caught up in the frenzy where I thought gold wouldn't go much higher even with a bad economy. This was in the seventies. Now looking back, I realize what a real mess we are in. Think about it; if we have a total collapse, house prices can retreat to what they were in 1972 even with our devalued currency. This is really scary. Food would cost more than housing, and energy? Forget it. Rub two sticks together to keep warm and hope your mistress doesn't mind living in a cardboard box from Sears.

Back now to Enoch. It seems God put some people on earth only to decide that they are too noble to walk among the rest of us and he takes them away. Enoch was such a person. He understood the concept of time, so he must also have understood the concept of money and greed, not by his being greedy, but by watching the effect money had on other people. God must have put great value in Enoch's opinions for the angels to grab him and take him up to heaven to plead the case for some wayward angels brought before God.

One of the reasons why I am including religion is that religion, along with money, is pretty much responsible for all the wars that have gone on during the centuries; so to see where we are going, we have to look at where we have been.

In the *Vita* and the Bible, greed started with Cain, but I think the real reason he killed Abel wasn't because God accepted Abel's sacrifice more but because of it; Adam and Eve were going to give their daughter Wioma to Abel to take for a wife when Cain was in love with her. Cain probably ended up taking her with him when he founded the city of Nod because we read no more about her. No doubt if they had children, they would have Cain's traits. I think that the flood must have dealt with his offspring. We know from the flood that Noah and his family were the only survivors, or were they? What about the Mayans in the mountains? Noah was a righteous man and so were his sons. The problem with greed is unless there is someone to warn you about it, it will creep up on you; and before you know, it has you hook, line, and sinker. So after a few generations of not training your children you are destined for problems.

I know I keep moving back and forth in time. I want you to get a sense of the journey because I am seeking an unbroken chain of greed. It seems greed dies with the person, so how does it get carried forward?

Uh-oh, we forgot about the Cruel One. I don't like to give any prominence to the devil, so I call him the Cruel One because of all the trouble and death that he has caused. Why give him any fame? He belongs in prison (lake of fire), and for my money (pun on words), one thousand years isn't long enough. It seems goodness and generosity are the only things that can counteract greed, so I guess when we are generous for the sake of being human; we are doing ourselves a favor. Greed is something we should guard against at all cost with prayer or reflection.

Money doesn't really appear as a driving factor until we start seeing kings; with kings come taxes. Israel didn't have any taxes until Saul. Sampson, the last of the judges, forbade taxes. You remember Sampson: he was always fighting the Philistines; only the Philistines were really Greeks that immigrated to the Middle East after God sank one of their islands because of immorality. God sent them to the land of Abraham because Jacob abandoned it to go to Egypt to be with Joseph, which probably made God angry. It seems God always takes peoples that do abominations and uses them to discipline Israel when Israel doesn't follow the statues, commandments, and accepts his judgments only to later have Israel smash them to pieces when Israel regains favor with God. What's coming in our time is that the Assyrians of the north—we call them Germans—will finance the Assyrians south of Israel, along with others, to fight with Israel. Of course, God will intervene; eventually smashing all of Israel's enemies; but God will only intervene after Israel follows the instructions in the book of Daniel. But this war between God and Israel's enemies will leave a big mess in the Middle East for quite some time. They will literally be putting markers by piles of bones to be buried years after the battle ends.

This is the end of this chapter, but bear in mind that everything that is going on now has its roots in religion (or the lack of it), greed, and the solution of the problem, which is God. What makes me uneasy in some ways is that the Assyrians descended from Shem, the third son of Noah. Noah and his sons found favor with God. I would have hoped that the entire people of Shem would be blessed, but it seems God has individual covenants with certain people, and only those people seem to be (most) important in the way God deals with man. Christ has an open-ended covenant with all that accept him. It seems the more spiritual someone is, the less likely they are to be greedy—just an observation on my part.

CHAPTER 2

How did banks begin? The modern-day beast that we have to deal with today was a benign pet that had its birth in assaying gold money and minting coins along with providing safe and secure storage of other people's money. After a while, the bankers realized that they could increase their profit potential by loaning out (other people's money) for interest without telling the person who owned the gold, and as long as everyone didn't want their gold all at the same time, the banker would be safe. *This is surely greed.* There are no good points to speak of in speaking of greed except to say that you could flatten the pointy nose of the banker if you could catch him. Eventually, the cat got out of the bag, and a run on the bank occurred; people were mad, but bankers—being as slippery then as they are now—Helicopter Ben as an example, bankers then offered to pay interest on whatever money you put in the bank (unlike now), and the people accepted this.

People with a lot of money realized that they could open a bank and make even more. Greed seems to be contagious once infected. Things really became interesting after the plague; all those people dying, leaving their money and property to the next of kin sparked the Renaissance period that brought science, art, and learning to the forefront. These things distracted the attention just like the gladiators did in Rome and MTV and *Star Search* do today, so the bankers are free to strip us naked and rape us. Greece is getting it now. What a shame; they once ruled the world. We are next.

Anyway, back to the Italian Renaissance and the major banking families. I'm not going to swear to it, but I think the women really controlled the banks in Italy because only women kill with poison, and the dead from poisoning littered the streets ten to one as compared with male sword fights and intrigues. The male courts retaliated. To this day, a husband can kill his wife, and seven years is the most they can keep him in jail—such morbid goings-on in Italy these days. One can't tell whether or not the president is a part-time (pimp)? And if so ,is it because he likes the work or he needs the money, but Italy soon got beaten out by the Germans' Bauer, who changed their family name to Rothschild, I'm told or research suggests. Remember now, Germans are really Assyrians. From my research, these people are very alert, industrious, and energetic about making money and advancement. Beer was invented by the Assyrians long before the Common Era, which means before the birth of Jesus Christ, so they have had plenty of time to become experts at making it.

The Rothschild's were not so as ingenious as most people think. They just followed the banking method of the Templars with notes of credit instead of transporting large sums of money around to be stolen by thieves. Here's the thing to keep in mind: In the past, thieves had to keep changing the game. Every time they would get caught, people were made aware of what they were doing, and law enforcement went on the prowl for them. It used to be that way; these days, bankers keep doing the same thing over and over again. Madoff, I think, is at the pinnacle for greed in our current times, and folks, had he been tried a couple of years later, he would not have gone to jail because they passed laws protecting this sort of behavior if it is done a certain way. But Bernanke takes the prize, I think, for all time in what I think to be the biggest banking conspiracy concerning corporations. Yes, we are a corporation.

CHAPTER 3

We stopped being a sovereign nation back in the 1930s, but I'll talk more about this further on in the story; back to the great-granddaddy of bankers (if this book doesn't blow the transmission of your mind first, you will survive what's coming). The money changers took banking to a new level, global for their period of time. They would finance both sides of wars and saw to it that the losing side didn't default on its debt. Let's see if they still have that kind of power. Iceland defaulted and they are still here. Hm, bankers then made use of every single technology like they do today. In their day, the most up-to-date communications was to have two men on each horizon, about twenty miles away from each other, with lanterns at night and a sort of Morse code. It was much faster than riders carrying the messages. Anyway, they put it to good use. From what I have gleaned from different sources, when Napoleon Bonaparte lost at Waterloo, a false message was sent, saying that Napoleon won and Wellington lost. The stocks in London fell. The people in the know bought up all the stocks for pence on the pound, and when the truth finally came in that Wellington won and Bonaparte lost, stocks went soaring. The bankers got richer, and the middle class disappeared. Sound familiar? Forgive me if I have a keystroke error; I didn't mean to hit an *M*. No sooner had Wellington won his victory; the European bankers seated in London decided to take back the United States. They had battle-seasoned British regulars fresh from Waterloo attack us, and on with the war of 1812.

Let's look at the United States in that period and a little before. Say, let's start with A little prior to the war for independence, the United States had very little capital cash reserve—none to be exact. We didn't coin money per se; we used a mishmash of British and Spanish money.

We did have one thing: an abundance of *goodwill* and trust in each other, so we developed the goodwill script. Each state created its own. It had no value like today's money and everyone knew it, but they gave it value in exchange for goods and services. The bankers across the pond saw this and immediately tried to put a stop to it. This and other offenses triggered the war, but they were persistent because after the Revolutionary War (plus ten years), the European bankers pushed for a central bank. Jefferson warned of it, but they got their charter. Now with their bank in place and Wellington's victory, the bankers felt safe in attacking us, figuring they had us by the throat, and in comes the war of 1812. They didn't figure on the resolve of the American people, so after so many more bloodied noses and lost battles, the bankers finally realized—since they burned the capitol and most of Washington—they could make peace, knowing the United States was broke and we would have to go to them for money to rebuild. They could still win the game, only in another way. This is why the war came to an end prior to Jackson beating the British at New Orleans.

Their revised plan was for a French arm of the bankers to loan us money or, should I say, give us the money, to rebuild Washington with one condition: an architect of their choosing would lay out the city, and they had some design, a revised design from their first design. Oh, you didn't know after the original war started in 1776 that ended in 1785, we were broke? The Continental currency was not as inflated as it is today, but it was bad, so French bankers came to our aid and presented us with an offer. They would supply the money, and we would use their architect and their design for the layout of the city. This is how they forced us into accepting a central bank the first time. The design created a demonic antenna, attracting every unclean spirit, and this is why Washington is as corrupt as it is. Crazy idea, maybe, but there are a lot of books out there that say the same thing.

What threw a wrench into their gearbox was old Jackson himself. He threw out the central bank by not renewing their charter in the 1830s. It seems as much as Jackson and Jefferson disliked each other, they loved this country; and Jefferson pointed out what was going on, and Jackson, at his first chance, acted on it. Jackson only got elected once, but he was extraordinarily honest. Once, while on the capitol steps, a uniform maker offered him a bribe to get the contract to make the Continental army's uniforms. Jackson grabbed him and threw him down the steps and kicked him. We sure could use that type of honesty in Washington now as a general rule instead of the exception.

Greed didn't really seem to be a factor among the masses. They were content to be on their own, and as long as there was food on the table and a smile in the baby's eyes, the average American was happy. What made this country great was the fact that we were able to keep what we made and were able to spend the money any way we pleased. Our needs were simple, and our religion was plain Bible-based religion and a tolerance for things different from ourselves as long as we could understand what was being said. We were, for the most part, fulfilled. We won our freedom with nothing to hold us back. Men could dream without fear, and their thoughts and aspirations would become the reality of invention—inventions of all types. With these inventions came wealth, and with wealth came greed and back again. What I've noticed about greed, besides it being contagious, is it tends to cause people to seek out other people of the same circumstance, whether out of fear because the poor might ask for money and other rich people would not, or because they felt that they were better from other people now that they have become rich. I saw a movie about the *Titanic* where the conversation was about old money versus new money. Greed is greed although, as of late, I have noticed some extremely wealthy people giving their money away; a positive thing, for their wealth is in the billions, and how much can one man spend in a lifetime? Some people have a sincere desire to leave the world a little better because of living than a little worse. To these noble people, we are all thankful, I'm sure.

Back to the 1830s, we can't talk about greed without talking about slavery. Probably the worst kind of greed is not the greed for money but the greed to be able to control the lives and destinies of other people. I have always found the people of the South to be very kind and gracious regardless of circumstance, so why were the slaves in many cases treated so badly? The only thing that I can liken it to is people when they get behind the wheel of a car. Ever notice how their personality changes? The power, the control behind the wheel—people who enjoy bumping cars are an extreme example of this. Give someone—anyone—power over another person, and sooner or later, you're in for trouble. Slavery is a human example. What freed the black people wasn't the white abolitionists alone; it was their simple prayers like the Hebrews in Egypt, praying to God for the 450 years they were in slavery. God gave the Hebrews Moses, and God gave the slaves Lincoln after 350 years of prayer.

A modern-day version of power breeding greed is a lawyer who steals the estate of a little old lady. It isn't greed alone, but the power over someone else with the thought of getting away with it is probably what makes it happen. Nowadays, thievery is rampant, so let's return to the 1830s for a while.

I'm sorry for bouncing you back and forth in time like this, but perspective can only be achieved by continuous comparison of the subject matter and the medium. Like a painter holding his thumb before himself and the canvas, we need perspective.

By the time we get to the actual cash manipulations, you will be prepped. So it's the 1830s. Jackson's in the White House and the American people are proud. We are starting to move westward—the Louisiana Purchase of 1803 and the 1836 Republic of Texas—a very exciting time. Still there is very little overall greed. Vast fortunes are being made, but people seem to count their blessings. Greed starts to creep in again in 1848; Joseph Glidden invents barbed wire, and the plains are no longer free or open. Gold is discovered in Sutter's Mill in 1848, spurring the gold rush of 1849.

Interestingly, people were used to working hard all day long for a meager pay and were content; now, the thought of bending down to pick up enough gold in one day to live like a king for the rest of their lives had people all wound up. I call this innocent greed—the same type of greed people have when they buy a lotto ticket and dream of winning. This innocence lasts only as long as it takes for the ticket to be a winner. Like a gold strike, everything changes. A winning ticket, a gold strike—they bring out the worst and most aggressive nature in man. *Not good.* The nobility of man blows out the window when the gold dust blows in. The gold did one very important thing: it sparked a homegrown industrial, manufacturing investment spree. We no longer needed foreign seed capital; we had our own now, and it came from California. Capital investment grew along with industry, and unfortunately, greed went along for the ride. All this growth didn't go unnoticed. Our friends, the bankers, had been watching our rags-to-riches climb, and they wanted their unfair share of the pie; so they sat down and thought necessity was the mother of invention. So they would create a financial panic, and then they innocently volunteered to bail us out. A half-a-dozen times of bailing out the nation and we would be begging to have a central bank. Actually, what gave them the idea was a shipload of gold from California on its way to New York that sank in the 1850s, the USS *Central America*, which caused a panic at the exchange.

In the past, the incoming immigrants were a blessing. They brought expertise along with the sweat of their brow. They, for the most part, were honest; and all they wanted was an opportunity. They understood that they had to learn to speak English and abide by our laws. Now it seems what used to be our strength is being turned against us. Instead of contributing more than they take, they take more than they contribute, but is that greed? My mother always said refusers are losers, but even in her generation, she knew that to take unfair advantage of a situation was wrong.

As it seems, we have bred a current-day master that likes to take from the rich and give to the poor. Some say he wasn't bred here, so he has no sense of loyalty, but I will always say that our founding fathers had much greater wisdom than ourselves. Mainly for them, it resulted in their death for a difference of opinion without recourse. For us today, the road forks, becoming diverse. One way waters the tree of liberty, a sad end or fresh start; the other path is less certain, fraught with danger. Only someone with the instilled trust of a Washington and the diplomacy and directness of a surgeon could restore us in time. Let's see what 2012 brings. I have hopes, which we will explore further on. I wrote a poem for each war our nation has suffered through, along with a built-in honorarium to either a person or a group.

Valley Forge

Farmers, tinsmiths, tinkers all
They've been there since early fall

An infant nation guard laments
Of cold, food, and circumstance

Icicles fall as if they were tears
Sympathy as if winter cares
The war can go on for years

Snow, waist-high
Every day more die
On Washington we do rely

Hair white as snow, eyes ablaze
Nothing ever seems to FAZE

This warrior we choose to follow

The English are camped across the river
Plotting, planning, it makes me quiver

So much depends on our success
Life, liberty, and happiness

I remember what one man professed
At gallows' gate before he died

Give me liberty or give me death
To these sentiments we all attest
We are resolved to do our best

Back to the 1850s, the telegraph had been in service for a while, and it changed many things especially for the bankers in Europe. It gave them an even bigger edge. Back here, we were expanding new states, adding all the time; and the biggest issue of the time was, will a state come in as a slave state or a free state? You would think with the invention of the cotton gin that the slave trade would diminish. Not so. They did away with slavery in 1836 in England; you would think we would have taken the hint, but profit from slaves was big. Greed got to be bigger, a real monster now.

I remember in high school, we had a library with stuff going way back, personal accounts of people. I used to love to read those—diaries, newspapers, all sorts of stuff. The laws were strict about the sales of slaves—miscegenation, all sorts of stuff—that would make a person with a conscience sick at what was legal for blacks. Plantation owners could sell a child and split the family, and it was legal. Freed slaves with papers had rights, but even then, things were uncertain if you strayed away from family. I found a diary in our school library that talked about a woman and husband that moved to Tennessee and disappeared; her marriage name was Fields. I remember reading and feeling grief of the person who wrote the diary. The writing was blurry in some spots, which leads me to think whoever wrote it was crying at the time. I read she was sold back into slavery; her husband was killed, and she died during childbirth. The person who wrote the diary was a former slave, I think. The record of the date was 1833, which were the slave days still. How did the person who wrote the diary learn to read? It was a crime then to teach a slave to read; anyway, to take a free person and sell them back into that kind of situation was *pure greed*. For some, the civil war was a money-making environment that even the most pious could not resist. Everything from blockade runners to cheaply made goods sold at extremely high prices. They called the people who made their money this way the shoddy aristocracy. Those people should have felt shame, but the power of greed drowned out any voice of conscience they might have heard, leaving the situation to continue till the end of the war.

War always brings forth new inventions—better ways to kill in order to exercise greed. History repeats itself. I have a better idea; instead of exercising greed, let's exorcise it. This way, instead of money being a god to some, it would be no more than a system of exchange.

I know it must be trying for the reader bouncing back and forth like this, but once we hit the 1900s, I will follow a pattern that will be much easier for the reader to follow. I think that you have been conditioned enough. I wrote a poem about Lincoln that, I think, sums up what he must have suffered, having to deal with generals, war profiteers, protagonistic senators, and congressmen of the period.

Lincoln

Features befitting a lowly man

Eloquence owned by a king

Wrinkles mark the skirmishes

The war will be over by spring

His gate belies a destiny

In that only time will tell

As a pen moves a nation and a sword removes a foe

Justice either way is only for GOD to know

Stern eyes reveal the pain

A nation through shot and shell

For a country to bury its dead

For him a living hell

In speaking he was heard to have said

In remembering the dead

That the ground has been made sacred

More than what can ever be read

With this his destiny comes to a close

His light goes out with a flash

And now when we remember him

His body is only ash

Lincoln was one of those noble people that only by the grace of God found his destiny. Sad as his end was, where would we be had he not been president? I believe that he knew what his fate was and was resigned to embrace it. A week or so before his death, a photo was taken and the plate cracked with the line going through his head; he took it to be an omen, but the battle that kept him up at night with horror was Shiloh.

Shiloh

Trumpets sound, men abound
Some in blue, the rest in gray
One in the clearing, the other in the fray
Pitted against each other in this way

Hear the shouts, the awful screams
These are the sounds that war brings
Thunder of cannon, then the rain
To wash the ground clean again
Battle continues into the night

Morning breaks, men abound
Dead and wounded litter the ground
Some in blue, the rest in grey
Were they fell is where they'll stay
Wooden crosses mark the way
To SHILOH

Wars in the past didn't breed as much greed as they do today. The money spent on our military prowess is the envy of all; well, at least it used to be. Let's get up-to-date. Since our financial difficulties, other countries have seen their chance and have grabbed it. China is enlarging its army and navy with the same look the Japanese had when they went into Manchuria; only with China, it will be Taiwan without even firing a shot—Tibet all over again. Greed has no boundaries; it lacks conscience or foresight, and it continues to feed on the poor and the elderly until checked by the indignation of the brave without which there would be no hope.

America, land of the free, home of the brave; was it bravery that recently let a man's house burn down because he forgot to make a payment to his local fire department? Nope. It was greed. Ben Franklin instituted the very first volunteer fire department. Even Roosevelt's analogy to lend-lease policy made allowances for loaning his neighbor a hose to put out a fire as long as he got the hose back in good repair.

I am an ardent constitutionalist; I believe the time has come to stay in our own backyard and let God take care of things. The Bible even says so in Daniel; it talks about a beast with the head of a lion and the heart of a lion. The lion's face is replaced with the face of a man, and a man's heart is given to it, and the eagle's feathers are plucked. Old Teddy Roosevelt was an American lion as an example of American interventionism, but Teddy only struck after he was hit, same as Franklin, and not before. I guess WMDs are a worry. Times change and people stay the same, or do people change and history repeats itself?

Now back to the 1870s post-Civil War and the reconstruction period—probably the saddest, vilest time in our country, for as a whole, we descended upon a beaten South; and instead of helping them, we sought every opportunity to displace them.

People make plans and God laughs. All it takes is one Jonah on a ship for the ship to be lost, and there was a ship; it was called the USS *Tennessee*. During the post-Civil War, it carried passengers from New York to the South. On one such trip, northern investors sought to make a fortune investing in the collapsed markets of the South and, therefore, loaded barrels of gold on board the *Tennessee*; and on its way, a hurricane hit and the *Tennessee* went down.

This is why one should never seek to make money on the misery of others. It's happening today—modern-day profiteers—only it is in the foreclosure market, in housing. What are we becoming, or what have we already become? It's like the return of the robber barons. Jay Gould could bankrupt a company with just the rumor that he was going to buy a stock, and yet with all the goings-on and none of the safety nets of what we have today, no one really starved. Back then, though, we didn't pay farmers not to grow things; a farmer used his land the way he saw fit and that is as it should be. There was no greed in the farmer of the 1800s; there was a lot of satisfaction though. It didn't matter how a farmer planted his field; God made it productive. Now it's the big combines and big money. Greed takes center stage. A person like Edison, who was a better businessman than inventor, made millions; and Tesla, a better inventor than a businessman with so much to give, dies broke, feeding pigeons. Where is the justice in that?

We, the people, allowed these things to happen; so in a sense, we got what we deserved. With all the greed swirling about you, someone would step up to the plate, like a young David, to do battle with the Goliaths; and so he did. Teddy Roosevelt was our David. His first Goliath was the Northern Securities Company, which he broke up with the Sherman antitrust laws, and others followed. Teddy loved people; the more different they were from himself, the more he enjoyed them, and he loved to eat. He was the salt of the earth and the farthest you could get from a NWO type. Anything Teddy did, he did in the best interest of the people. He hated bankers; he sent Kermit off to war in 1917. He died in France. He would not have sent him off had he thought there was foul play. Buried alongside Kermit is Theodore Jr., winner of the Medal of Honor. I wrote this for the marines in the style of a poet called Joyce Kilmer, who was killed in WWI.

Pride of the Marines

As I stand in my trench, dreaming of home

A shell awakens me, I'm all alone

My buddies lie around me, cold and dead
I'm all that's left to go on ahead

Why do they call this place Labella Wood?
There are no trees, only splinters of wood

The cold below or the fire above
I have no love for either one

It's hard to imagine there ever being trees
There's nothing to shelter me from the bite of the breeze

I gaze down at my feet, two blocks of ice

A strange sense of warmth is coming over me

I cannot feel below my waist
My pulse quickens

I must make haste
Our Father who art in heaven

Had Teddy been president instead of Wilson, there would not have been a Federal Reserve or income tax. He would have hung them from a tree. Wilson was a quiet man, extremely well educated. He was a true idealist who was misled, and in the end, the grief of it gave him a stroke. It wasn't so much the failure of the fourteen points as much as he realized what a monster was created with the new banking system. He was sometimes labeled as a NWO-type person, but he wasn't. He meant well, and as usual, well-meaning people with the best of intentions always seem to cause the biggest problems. He got reelected with the slogan he kept us out of war, but we ended up involved. Munitions manufacturers, before we even got into the war, were having a field day. Companies like DuPont made so much money during World War I mainly because they were the only large chemical company that could deliver explosives in any great quantity. They made even more money during World War ll, making explosives for the Manhattan project.

The Day a President Wept

A shot in the east that brought fire to the
West
Four years a nation in waiting
To take not a bride in peace but a mate in
War
A fire to consume some, a cloud to confuse the rest
A man like any other man, he carries the weight of the world
On his shoulders
His pen controls the posterity of a nation
A land where each man pledges to defend
The rights of all other men
Brooding over the last full measures of devotion while
Gazing over pillared fields where flowers once grew
Yielding to the all-consuming ever-increasing cries
Of the people
Cajoled
By the people
Signed, bowed his head, and cried
For the people

WOODROW WILSON
A SANE MAN FLOUNDERING IN A SEA OF INDIFFERENCE

I think that if Wilson were alive today, he would not
approve of what the UN has become.

CHAPTER 4

Let's talk about what I believe to be the designing criteria for the Federal Reserve.

Everyone wants to get rid of it. I agree, but being a scientist, I felt compelled to dissect it and study it. Their records are secret. Congressman Ron Paul of Texas has been trying to pry the steel door open for years; and now with the help and support of the courts and other congressmen and senators, he will succeed, I think, but this can take a while. I am an impatient person sometimes, so I thought of how to figure out what makes the Federal Reserve tick. We know, through various sources, who put it together and what they have done, but we know little of its inner workings. The Glass-Steagall Act put the beast under some form of control, and in order to do that, someone inside must have given the senators confidential information as to its ultimate goals—one of which is now apparent to me, which was to bankrupt the country. As proof of this, let's look at the currency; the largest denomination on an American note pre-1916 was $100. Post-1928, we see them test print a Woodrow Wilson $100,000 bill. They said the bills were solely for credit between banks. One need only look at Zimbabwe money and think, *Glass-Steagall stopped a lot of things.* I think Teddy Roosevelt headed us in the right direction, and the Federal Reserve was a way to sidestep laws the banks would have to follow and any future laws regarding banking and business. So to see the inner workings, we need to look at what they were trying to avoid. I think mainly it was to avoid banking monopoly laws and certainly to avoid corporate taxes not just here but the whole world, but for that, they needed the ability to avoid disclosure. That's being stripped away as we speak. They had to access the power to exert capital control on more than one nation without the nation knowing it. It had to have the ability to continually remove current production of global gold reserves from the open market, leaving a token for a small percentage of investors and jewelry so as not to lead the masses to believe that enough gold was available to use as a form of hard currency. It seems, with its insatiable thirst for power and driven by *greed*, I now believe that the Federal Reserve was designed as a platform for a total takeover of the duties of all the main US courts and all the government agencies, including the functions of Congress and the Senate.

Oh boy, time for another game. I want to condition you first. Women, as a rule, mature faster than men; they have to. If they are not running away from some men, they are riding a bike for whatever reason they give. Most will understand what I'm about to say. Remember how tricky algebra was? Derivatives are a form of math one step trickier than algebra. Give the expertise of this science to the reprobate minds of Wall Street, and you have created a financial instrument that can be doubly sold just like the slave that I talked about earlier in the book. To understand the derivative is to understand a puzzle ring. A formula created it, and along with the formula is a key; you can uncreate it. Here's the problem: if I'm a bank and I created these securities, selling them as AAA–rated, at least some of their components have to be AAA, and the rest are set to collapse, bringing the derivative down. Only the people with the key can separate these derivative securities. See where I'm going with this? I sell the derivative for $100; after two years, it collapses, and I buy it back for 50 cents. I put it through the reverse formula and end up with both good and bad holdings, which can be separated. Now you know why everyone is scared to buy a foreclosed house. Remember what may happen to those that seek to gain through the misfortune of others who have rightful title to the mortgage.

Since we will probably never get the key formula for these securities, a law should be written, nullifying older mortgages and only accepting new mortgages since people who will buy these homes are buying in good faith and should get a good and clear title to the property. I've been watching from a distance. I like Elizabeth Warren. I think she is an honest woman, and she has been thrown into a den of pit vipers. It's not venom they impart into their victims; it's sort of a zombie-izing virus that leaves its victims numb and confused. The antidote for this zombie-izing virus is in the full and complete disclosure to Congress. See how the Department of Consumer Protection was ignored and superseded by a new agency placed inside the Federal Reserve to deal with the problem of mortgages? It's all about control now. Let's hope that they don't create any more agencies within the Federal Reserve. My worst nightmare is an agency assigned to the safety and production of goods in the United States. You know the first thing they would go after is gun production. If we ever lose the Second Amendment, we lose everything. Our founding fathers did things in order. The most cherished rights were apportioned to the First Amendment, and to forever stand vigilant, guarding over the First Amendment was the Second Amendment. I say that when it comes to greed, fear a government that fears the guns in the hands of the people.

Let's talk about the genius of the founding fathers before we go any further. We are talking about men who taught themselves how to speak Latin, French, and any other language that they needed to speak. They learned the sciences on their own. They drank mostly beer and wine because pure water was hard to keep, and many of them drowned the sorrows of lost loved ones. More people died young then than now. You are looking at very tempered, hardened-by-adversity type of people. We certainly can't claim that honor anymore.

I know women that cry when they break a nail and men who don't know what a screwdriver is, for back then, a farmer could fix anything with cutters and a roll of baling wire. Now, we have become soft. In the last one hundred years, they have made us lazy. How did they do that? Well, in devaluing the dollar, they forced people to unionize for more than just safe working conditions. Mass production produced cheap goods, so the banks said, "Why not make a profit from this by devaluing the currency a little?" It would make the prices of the products go up only slightly and no one would be the wiser. How can they do that, though, with the dollar tied to gold, any number of ways? I think in the beginning, they could sell bonds with a set yield tied to the dollar payable to them, which they probably did, or they could have laid plans very early on for the systematic separation of the dollar from gold, which becomes more evident over the years; but here's why I brought up the genius of the founding fathers: I think they anticipated something like this and put a sort of safety plug that could be pulled to stop this behavior cold in its tracks. I found it probably because God brought it to my attention. I think he brought it to the attention of Franklin Delano Roosevelt, and he kept it to himself, leaving it for a future generation to find and use in case our present situation ever occurred. I'm saving it till later; then I will explain it to you. Let's go back a little and talk about bonds. Who sells bonds anyway? Anytime I ever thought of a bond, it had something to do with a corporation, so if I buy a US savings bond, what kind of bond is that? As far as I'm concerned, it's sort of a corporate bond. It pays in general 5 percent, or it used to.

How can it pay 5 percent if the interest rate to borrow from a bank is 4 percent or lower and how can each stockholder of Federal Reserve stock get a 6 percent dividend? Well, when times were better and people had more faith in the economy, the country borrowed to pay it. It seems to me that the country should have borrowed the money from the bank that was charging 4 percent instead of borrowing the money from me and paying me 5 percent. I wonder who had the lion's share of bonds and what tax benefits were written into the law just for certain people.

So it seems to me we started to become a corporation in 1913 with the Federal Reserve Act of that year. Corporations in the United States were taxed unless tax exempt or they post a loss, but who would want a bank that was always showing losses to manage the affairs of a nation? I wouldn't, would you? How do you know whether or not they posted a loss? Perhaps their profits are reflective of the inflation rate. In that case, they have made a lot of money since 1913. If Jackson were still alive, every tree limb on the White House lawn would have a rope hanging from it.

Let's play a game, just a game. Let's say that each year; the money taken out of the US economy represented by the inflation rate was used to buy the lion's share of global gold production for that year. How much gold would that be? I would sure like to know where that money went, wouldn't you? Is it about gold, greed, or power? It's about power. Without the gold, you would have to take whatever medium of exchange they gave you to use, thereby giving them the power to start the game all over again; so you don't want paper money of any kind or a cashless society either.

My book is about greed. It seems that greed and power are maybe one and the same in some respects. I'm relaying this story to you in waves now in an effort not to put you to sleep but keep you thinking. What's going on now is a glorified version of the shell game, the shell game being the beginning of the Federal Reserve, and the glorified version is the financial products developed by mathematical engineers today. I think the engineers of Wall Street would have been better off developing a better rat trap for catching four-legged rats than giving new ways for the two-legged ones to steal. With the pre-Federal Reserve, there was no one place for money to flow into the market. The stock market was like the free market, where you can walk into a shop and buy a suit like you would buy a stock. Back then, though, because every sale was done by hand, it generally took two days for a transaction to be completed. Edison's ticker tape machine changed things a little, but not much. You see, one of their objects was to get the money to pass through the Federal Reserve (their Federal Reserve note) as a central bank, then to the market much the same way all other countries have to buy the US dollar before they can buy oil, but that's changing too, so the Fed was making money on both sides. I will say this for those old-time bankers: they knew how to turn a buck (no pun intended).

I noticed something cyclical about the whole existence of man from the ancient times till today, and I am sort of repeating it in the way I'm telling the story. That is, first, there is a period of immorality followed by a period of depression followed by a war to cleanse the land. Pick a period of time and try the theory out. Look, we had the roaring twenties followed by the Depression and then a world war. This pattern goes on all the way back to ancient times. I wonder if God has been trying to discipline us all this time. If so, with all the immorality we have had and the financial situation we are currently in, there is one giant war brewing someplace.

Since we brought up the 1920s, let's take a closer look. The Federal Reserve has now had seven years to flex its wings, daredevils are breaking records, Prohibition is on, and a feeling of "hey, if it feels right, do it" attitude started to permeate the American culture. The likes of Al Capone became a local hero when the Depression hit by helping feed the poor. His underground economy was generating something like $200,000,000 a year with alcohol that was tax-free along with other vices. Greed breeds extreme violence here since all of his revenues were in cash, and he kept it out of banks per se. The Fed found itself able to print money just so the people who wanted to shop would have some cash to do it with, so it's time to play another game—just a game mind you. Let's pretend someone got an idea. I think, *Why not do a bank emergency like the one in 1854, only we will do it with the market?* Morgan wouldn't need to cover the US government as he did in 1895. They would let the people stew in a depression till they could elect a president who knew how to get things done, but didn't understand money like Hoover did. They could then confiscate all the gold, replace it with paper, and whenever they needed money, they could print a percentage based on the amount that they knew was being kept out of circulation consistent with the underground economy (what an excuse to keep crime flourishing), and prices wouldn't change much. But their scheme backfired a little bit; one of the platforms Roosevelt had in his campaign was to repeal Prohibition, which he did. There was great deal of behind-the-scenes activity in this election, I'll bet. Anyway, Roosevelt gets in; he repeals Prohibition and starts his New Deal policy. I don't think Roosevelt understood money as much as he understood pallor snakes and the Constitution. It was his administration that faced the shortfall, so he finished what began in 1913, and I believe he incorporated the United States as an asset of the bank.

These are my thoughts: He smiled all the time and really wasn't worried. The bankers would rub their hands together not knowing that they made a mistake. To form a corporation from scratch is simple, but to dissolve a corporation and replace it with a new corporation is something entirely different. These are all my thoughts on paper, so don't believe anything I say. Check for yourself. The Constitution of the United States article VI reads, "ALL Debts contracted and Engagements entered into, before the Adoption of this Constitution, shall be as valid against the United States under this Constitution, as under the Confederation" (What does that mean to you?) I know what it means to me; it means that the United States is a corporation owned by the people. The Federal Reserve Act was passed when hardly anyone was in chamber. No due diligence was made to notify the stockholders (the American People that the United States was being dissolved). One sure way to check and see is to look at the minutes of Congress and see if they voted. To dissolve one corporation, the United States, under this Constitution before instituting a new one, a referendum would have been required to make it legal.

No referendum was put before WE the People to VOTE ON. *We* are still playing the game, so plan one failed. OK, no Prohibition, so plan two came into effect. They would confiscate gold at $20 an ounce, then reestablish the price of $34.50 an ounce to cover the shortfall, $14.50 an ounce.

I wonder how many total ounces were confiscated, and the bank got its money in gold. Gold and silver is the only real money among thieves; they horde it and bury it like pirate's gold. The only thing for honest people to do now is to demand gold and silver for true value and good delivery of assets in exchange for goods and services.

I can only imagine how many new technologies we would have if all these young engineers went into R&D instead of finance. Back in the old days, commodities were in a basket already or in silo of grain waiting to be shipped. Again, people plan and God laughs. They invented something called futures—probably the first mainstream Wall Street gambling invention that played on fate. Like the *Titanic*, we spit into the wind and God sent it back to us. Check out the dust bowl of the 1930s—God's stern warning because of the immorality of the '20s. There was no HARRP back then for your conspiracy theorists so explain it? Roosevelt knew only too well an idle hand and mind is an abomination to the Lord, so he did the only thing he could do. Back then, the banks tried to get him to allow what they are doing now, but he figured out their game; and with some help, he gave them Glass-Steagall Act instead. Also to combat it, he created work projects that would take people off the streets and away from criminal temptation, putting them to work enhancing the infrastructure. For the elderly, he created Social Security. He knew it wasn't constitutional, but the nation's back was against the wall and the people were scared. His fireside chats, his simple way of explaining complex problems, gave hope and comfort to the people along with Seabiscuit. To set the example, we—the people—would come back. He was as slippery a president as Lincoln, for friends as well as for foes, so the bankers hit a stone wall here. We see the perversity of the '20s and the Depression and barren land of the '30s; well, now comes the war—a big one according to their times. I think Roosevelt saw the bankers turn their attentions away from us temporarily, and they financed Hitler and his war machine. I think that this horrified Roosevelt. A real chess game ensued. He was stuck with a nation that was preoccupied in recovering from the Depression and a bank-mentored maniac bent on global suicide. Had we not fought World War II when we did, what reality would we be facing? I say all things happen for the best for those who believe in God.

This last war that is coming, I think the United States will stay out of because God himself will fight it when the time comes. Who is to know whether or not Roosevelt knew ahead of time that the Japanese would attack Pearl Harbor? It's a case of semantics now. Our entering the war was inevitable, so I leave the rest for God to know. My former department head, when I was in communications, was a radioman at Pearl Harbor during the attack; he saw the *Arizona* go up.

Arizona

Quietly she rests below
Rusting bow but still aglow
With memories of years ago

Bleeding oil from her holds
Like her children that rest below

They lie in state undisturbed
Till the day when they'll hear
The voice of eternity loud and clear
Read the muster and they shall appear

And they shall be as they were before
Transformed by the grace of the law
We will see them one and all

I can't imagine what it must have been like—the thought of being violated, feeling alone. For some it must have rendered them useless, while others—normally useless people—sprang into action. One thing was certain: the American people were as enraged as a man whose wife was violated. Greed here was sidestepped by the dollar-a-year man although I have no doubt he made money on the sidelines at every chance he could, yet his expertise and dedication proved a deciding factor in war production. The problem was and still is, but will be, diminishing in the future as the military industrial complex that we built shrinks. The United States borrowed a lot of money during WWII. A lot of factory workers got rich working overtime and holidays, and they and a lot of other people bought Liberty Bonds, stamps, and every kind of war-related financial instrument available at the time. About 80 billion dollars went into World War II—a drop in the bucket with today's crippled dollar value. When you think about it, our wealth and economy that was generated by WWII has long since run out, so now that we have gone through our savings and put our grandchildren in debt while we were having a good time, what do we do? Greed didn't put us in debt; greed generally makes people rich. No, it was that "if it feels right, do it" attitude, that sinner's attitude.

Hm, I had to think for a while. It wasn't me; I always controlled my spending. I can't mention names, but I have some friends who got divorced. They were happy; they had four children together. He made quite a lot of money at his job; he worked hard, I think. I don't know, and I am ashamed to ask, but I think one of his clients was a stockbroker. He got talked into investing all his money and took a mortgage out on his house to invest. He lost everything, including his wife, because he took to drinking. Is it greed to want to provide adequately for your family? Or is it greed to want to get there quick? Remember the lotto tickets and the 49ers. The saying "easy come, easy go" doesn't apply here because he worked hard for the money. The brokers that made the windfall have probably already spent the money. For him, it was probably easy come, easy go. Here is the *greedy* one, the culprit: The Glass-Steagall Act dealt with the way banks and investment houses did business; it separated them as it should be. Back in the '90s, they did away with Glass-Steagall instead of supplementing it with legislation, capping high-speed trading (requiring each trade a two-day waiting period between purchase and resale) and criminalizing computer-generated products. These, in my evaluation, are the cause of the very high volatility in the market. Instead of priming the pump as Roosevelt did, they pumped the well dry. We are dead in the water. I'm sorry folks; we can get rid of the Federal Reserve, but that will still leave us stripped to the bone.

This is depressing, so let's go back to the post-World War II era and see if we can find a way out. With the death of Roosevelt, Truman took over. He was a lot tougher than he looked even though he sold women's finery. He was a captain of artillery in WWI, and the bankers couldn't get around him. Salesmen know every trick in the book, and when he said the *buck* stops here, he meant it for the Fed and they knew it. There was an assassination attempt on him after he got out of office, and I wonder now about it.

Eisenhower was another difficult president for the bankers to deal with. He was from Kansas—one tough farmer type. It turned out to be a bloody Kansas for the bankers. He was the first among the presidents to see the danger the "corporate banker military industrial complex" type of control present in the nation, and he made his feeling known upon leaving office. Kennedy, as I see it, posed as much a problem for the bankers as he posed for himself. I'm not a fan of Camelot. To understand the man, we have to look into his breeding to some extent. Rose Kennedy, for the most part, must have been a saint. She lived over one hundred years, outliving many of her children, yet she kept her sanity and composure. Prayer, I believe, did this. Joe Kennedy was the opposite of her belief system. His many affairs are recorded for time and posterity. So JFK was a blending of the two; he wasn't greedy, and he was a child of privilege. They enjoyed spending money more than making it. His driving force was equality. Apparently, he was not afraid to confront the NWO and talk about them in speeches about secret organizations, which goes to his credit. What got him killed, I think, was the price of oil and the fact he didn't want to take the common man's money away from them, which was silver. What would have saved him? If he was faithful to his wife, God would have stood in front of him. There's been too much written about him for me to believe him faithful. A shame for us; he had it in him to end the Fed had he lived, but he died, and we lost the only real money we had left. We really can't look at stocks as money ever again since the Federal Reserve came into existence. The value of the stock hasn't been determined by its profits since 1920. In post-1920, the hype surrounding the stock and its daily sales numbers controlled the price along with the proper PR. Don't believe me? Look at the two decidedly different financial endings for Charles Mitchell and Jesse Livermore. Not all bankers were with the NWO—those that weren't were allowed to sink, and the other, when Glass-Steagall prevented him from gaming anymore, took his own life. I guess there is a thrill attached to greed for some. We need only look to review Bear Stearns, Merrill Lynch, and the Lehman brothers and reflect on Mr. Mitchell and then look at Goldman Sachs.

The only real assets now are gold for the rich and silver for the common man. We haven't talked about gold for a while, so let's become vulgar and talk about it. When they passed the law to confiscate gold, it was set up so that they needed to pass another law to repeal it but not to modify it. This means as Congress needed money, it modified the bill. The original bill was that for every dollar of gold we have on deposit, we would print that amount in paper money; however, that changed after a while. Congress changed it to a percentage. Eventually, come 1971, we were down to about *zip*, so Nixon took us off the gold standard. Who owns the gold in Fort Knox? I like Nixon; he got us out of Vietnam. I could have had lunch with him if I wanted to. His stockbroker was a good friend, but I didn't because of the way he left office.

Separating gold from the dollar totally like that stopped the embarrassment of rating the dollar in fractions of an ounce, but now, we can look someday for the Dow Jones to be valued in fractions of an ounce. What an embarrassment that will be for the American people. Watching the markets now make me think of a movie I saw years ago called the *Moneychangers*.

Here's something that happened at the same time as going off the gold standard in 1972 that gave me to pause and think. I wondered why the

Iranians hate us so much. I heard rumblings to the effect that when our oil companies first started to develop the oil reserves of Iran, they did it with the understanding that the Iranians would put their money in American banks, which they did. Then we bankrupted their holdings, leaving them broke. Is this true? Some say yes; some say no, but it would be a reason for why they were so mad at us back then. Going off the gold standard left us on a slippery slope until Reagan. He saw what was going on, and in 1986, he made it legal to own gold again. He even opened a mint at West Point to mint and sell both gold and silver coins. See how they are sought after now? Reagan's big mistake was not pulling the plug on the Federal Reserve. He had the popular support. I think the bank threatened to pull the plug on us like they did with the bailout. We would have been a lot better off had he tried. I can't remember now whether he was shot before or after he legalized gold. The farther a president gets away from the Camelot's moral lifestyle, the safer he will be, which brings us to the Clinton administration.

I can only imagine what must be going through the reader's minds here. My research suggests saying as little as possible. To my thinking, he was not responsible for the robust economy of that period unless you want to give him credit for the Internet marketplace. There is something odd though. I watched the performance of a comedian who said that Clinton was the closest they ever got to having a black president, and people broke out in laughter. Lincoln freed them; Johnson and Kennedy gave them civil rights. What did Clinton give them? I don't know; I might have missed something. With all the publicity he got, more welfare? What does welfare do except tell someone subconsciously that they are unable to work and earn an honest living? I say we are all created equal, and each one of us has to sell ourselves to the marketplace with our individual talents and skills. If you're good at what you do, someone will give you a chance.

Greed certainly accelerated during this period. I think the more we ignored the Constitution and gave way to political correctness, the more greed grew. The sucking sound Ross Perot warned about was just about done, draining away all the wage-paying jobs, leaving the middle class scrambling to make ends meet. Working two jobs just to keep a roof over one's head was not greed for the American people. We had become used to having things, conveniences, different kinds of electronic diversions, all comprised of silver. Had silver been at its true value, there would have been less electronics and probably more economically savvy people, but as it turned out, we fell into their trap.

Things in Life
The waking hours of each day
Filled with so much dismay

People running here and there
But never getting anywhere
Puts them in such despair

Searching for a better life
But all they find is grief or strife

Never taking the time to see
The best things in life
Are really free

CHAPTER 6

Are we truly a two-party system? I don't think so anymore. I like Bush; Bush stood in defense of the Second Amendment on one hand, and he passed the Patriot Act on the other. See what pressure can do? What about today? The Constitution is on trial for its life.

Death

Death, thief of flesh
Horror of flight
Who will you steal this night?
The old or the young
Strong or the weak
In war or at peace
Who will you visit?
To fill your quota keep
You know no holiday
You take no rest
Century after century
You've done your worst
Man has done his best?
One day, you'll see a mirror
And you yourself will rest

Terror and WMDs are a real threat because they do exist. Everybody knows it. Each superpower has them; each superpower has criminals in their government that would sell anything if the price was right. Let's look at weapons in general. When I was a kid, we had firecrackers. TNT Bomb was one brand. I used to get them from a beautiful girl I went to school with. I didn't mind overpaying, but like most things, I got duds; the fuse would burn, then nothing. These were chemicals—sulfur, saltpeter, and charcoal. Then there is the other kind of technology. This is the stuff God used in the big bang theory of creation. This stuff is not only actuated by physics or chemistry; it's spiritual. When man uses it, a demon is required to set it off; take the demon appointed to the devise away and the impetus is gone. No demon and you get a dud, so I don't really worry about them anymore unless new ones are made. But I do worry about the Patriot Act. Both the Democrats and Republican overall policies seem the same except for Ron Paul and ten other congressmen who probably see the same dangers I do. Strange how the Bible talks about a ten-nation confederacy in Europe. We, here, passed laws allowing ten governors to take control of all fifty states under FEMA in times of emergency, suspending the Constitution, which was never to be allowed. Read constitutional case law ex parte Milligan. In re Milligan, my book seems to be more about power now than greed. It seems, looking with perspective, greed becomes power when you get enough of it. That's probably why a lot of wealthy people in the past felt that they could do anything they wanted and get away with it. Money buys legality. This is changing too, I think. As money becomes more worthless, the risks become too great. When money becomes worthless, what becomes of greed? We are in the middle of it right now; it's called control. They don't have to hide anymore or really pretend that they are two separate parties. They will argue they are. It appears that nothing gets done, but in reality, everything needed to initiate capital control is present. I mean capital controls on a global basis, the engineered dismantling of America's assets. All that stands in their way is Ron Paul with ten or eleven other congressmen. I don't know how many senators, but I'm sure that there are a few. I don't worry about them. God stands in front of them because they haven't been corrupted by Washington, so God will protect them. For those of you who don't know what capital controls mean, in effect, you lose private-property rights. They can freeze bank accounts, freeze foreign assets, and nationalize private pension funds; they can confiscate safety-deposit boxes. Now you know why they are tax deductible. I think Ron Paul threw a monkey wrench into their gearbox, forcing them to create a lot of Czars to sidestep Congress, and when that didn't work, they tried to swell the authority of the Federal Reserve in order to take over the government with a financial COO rather than a military one, though they are prepared for martial law. The only way that I see this situation as not ending badly is to unwind everything in a set order; that means the people will have to understand everything that's going to happen and be ready for it. They made money worthless, so we have to turn to them. We have to do the opposite. To beat greed, we will have to become, to some extent, the people we were in 1774. As an example, we will have to do Roosevelt in reverse. When Roosevelt created the CCC, he accomplished multiple things:

1. He got the young men off the streets, reducing crime.
2. They sent money home, helping spur the economy.
3. He prepared an army. He knew, in 1934, when the bankers turned their attentions to Europe, what was going to happen; so he took the young American men and made them strong and capable of taking orders.
4. He repaired the damage due to poor farming practices of the dust bowl, thereby reinvigorating food production in the United States.

What I'm saying is, each thing done to repair the nation was to have multiple beneficial effects; otherwise, the time it takes for the nation to recover will be longer. Doing nothing would have starved the nation. Starving the nation is what we have been set up for now. Look at our grain futures, sold abroad—if there will be any to sell with the crazy weather we've been having. What would happen if the places we buy our food from don't accept the dollar anymore and our homegrown food has been contracted abroad?

CHAPTER 7

First, I urge everyone to read Patrick Henry's famous speech to the Virginians. It could have been written against the banks instead of the Brits. Now I submit this question to you: Since the course of a nation relies totally upon the nobility of the men that occupy it, we are, alas, bankrupt. Integrity has flown from our nation's bosom, and deceit has replaced it, yet there is still a God in heaven to turn to for a remedy. Shall we, as a nation, fall to our knees and ask God for divine providence and to secure our liberty for us, or should we just boldly take back our country in his name in 2012? This is the question. Remember that indignation for what is going on is not enough; we need righteous indignation to be able to succeed, and for that, we need the blessings of an Almighty God.

I Like France. We learned something from the French during the Revolutionary War that they themselves have forgotten. The French in their Hundred Years' War was being beaten badly till Joan of Arc showed up. She showed them how a virtuous army could succeed. Now France faces a different sort of enemy, and again, only Joan's way will succeed; so in the future, don't be surprised if the Parisian way of the present-day France gives way to the Christian renewal brought on by prayer with a modern-day Joan of Arc, where Islam peacefully leaves France to return to the Arab nations.

In our present situation, things are set up so nothing will get done except possibly sound money, but that won't save us. The election in 2012 is our last chance. I saw a film called *Inside Job 2010* produced in Hollywood. Unlike other films coming out of Hollywood, it exposed what is going on in the government. I remember the voice of the narrator. His subdued tenor bothered me. He's probably asking himself questions about the future of the nation and wondering why more films are not made exposing this situation. I can't help but feel that he's having a crisis about whether or not he or Hollywood has a right to free will and the exercise of it. Perhaps for them, free will is like fame—an illusion. Here is who we need and why:

Ron Paul as president—he is the only one that can be trusted to put the Constitution back in the center of government and return us to a free market system. There is too much for one man to accomplish, so we need a working vice president with an expertise in business. Ross Perot comes to mind; he could use that expertise to reverse the vacuum that sucked away all those manufacturing jobs. Don't let his advanced age scare you; all he needs to do is snap out his orders to the people he trained, and they will do the work.

Peter Schiff for treasury secretary—we need to have a person at this post who understands economics and isn't afraid to say *no*.

James Turk to head the US mint; he understands money.

Jim Maloney to head the Bureau of Weights and Measures—we need an honest man to oversee the purity of the coinage.

Jim Rogers as commerce secretary—we need someone there that takes the same advice that he gives.

Marc Faber as the president's financial adviser—he has an uncanny ability to assimilate facts and figures in his mind and project future economic trends. I know what he will say though: do an honest default to get out of debt as soon as possible before you will be able to build real wealth again.

In speaking of trends, Gerald Celente to preside over Wall Street or what's to be left of it. Wall Street will have to be rebuilt because the Asian and Russian markets have opened their own exchange to compete with Wall Street.

Max Keiser as SEC head—who is better qualified than him to analyze and make assessments of financial products coming into the financial marketplace?

And finally—and as important as the president because to ensure the blessings of liberty, we first need the blessing of God—I searched, sought, and finally found a man that wants God's approval rather than man's. He has to correct us when we are wrong and not praise us, a man who will tell us what we need to hear rather than what we want to hear—Dr. Roderick Meredith of the Living Church of God. He is neither Catholic nor Protestant; he is what we had when we first started this nation—just a basic Bible-preaching scholar who has a fear and reverence for God, which is needed to ensure he leads us down the moral path and not the garden path. We have to have a balance. It would be folly to return to the Constitution while still having a nation bent on corruption. We need to reform our minds, work ethic, and moral code of behavior. We need to return to the people we were in 1776. At the same time this is going on, we need to eliminate the Federal Reserve and all of its support agencies, followed by an honest default and a new hard currency issued by Congress—this is really our only way.

When you consider all the money we gave away to other countries and never got back and all the help we gave the world over the years, not to mention all the money taken by inflation over the years, the money we owe China can be paid back on a gamble to avoid a war. I often wonder how much of our technologies they made off with without paying royalties or of a sensitive nature, yet we did borrow money from them. We can't ask others to be honest and pay their debts while we default on foreign debt. Grant the Chinese mineral rights to government land of their choosing for a period of time, the Chinese agreeing to repair the land as they go along—this would eliminate our debt to them. The Japanese, I'm sorry to say, no longer have a home to return to. In time, that whole island will be as hot as a witch's hat. We can roll over the debt we owe them into homes held in foreclosure. The Japanese can come here, but their immorality can't; it stays behind. In the meantime, restore the Constitution to its rightful place along with the congressional and senatorial powers we once enjoyed. The benefits of (limited government) greed is something man will have to learn to struggle with, but like in the '30s when everyone was in the same boat, it gets easier. In order to save ourselves, we will have to avoid greed. (Can a sparrow fall from a tree without God knowing it or can a nation rise without his help?) (Quote Ben Franklin) We have ignored God, and now he is ignoring us except for the lost tribes of Israel, which dwell among us. This is what my research shows.

I have to talk to you about something that I was going to leave out but am compelled to talk about it. In 1617, at Virginia Beach, Virginia, a cross was planted and a covenant with God was instituted that this nation was to be a Christian nation. Everything since then has been a struggle. Why do you think? Well, because in declaring it to be a Christian nation, we said that the land was going to be governed by the laws of God and not the Cruel One, and since then, he has been working to break the United States. The first thing the Cruel One did was to change the entry point into the United States from Virginia to New York; then he placed the Statue of Liberty in New York Harbor. We think the Statue of Liberty is to welcome new immigrants, but what it really is, is a statue of the whore of Babylon, telling people who understand to pay homage to her. The French people are not responsible for this; the bankers are. Unfortunately, New York is the new Babylon, and I fear for all that live there. The other thing is that our Declaration of Independence and Constitution had their conception in Philadelphia, which got its name from the Bible—the

Church of Philadelphia, which was faithful to God. So in order to corrupt the government, they had to move it, so they created DC, which soil is not consecrated to the original covenant with God. DC, for the most part, was a swamp where demonic sacrifices were held; it helped prepare it for what was to come. I really think that Washington should be abandoned and the capital should be returned to Philadelphia for the good of all. Some of our congressmen, out of fear during a wedding reception, came together in private and decided, in 1892, to declare this a Christian nation and did it, hoping to undo what was done earlier; but by then, the corruption was too great. I realize that—in telling you what I just did—it may jeopardize the credibility of everything else that I have said; but in order to put a puzzle together, you need all the pieces. If you are wondering why prices rise and salaries fall, it's because they need a level, stable global platform for the values of goods and services according to their needs—filet mignon for them, Oscar Mayer for us, and I don't mean Washington's Weenie .

Let's get back to money. Expect continuing capital controls, only now backed up by laws, forcing the banks to use pension funds, IRAs, 401(k)s, everything—even dormant accounts—to buy US treasuries because no one else wants them. Of course, with these laws, we have lost individual personal private-property rights. Now do you care about the Constitution? I'm sure now that I've caused all this emotional upheaval in you, the blowback of which will bounce around in your mind for a while—it will only be temporary with minor mental discomfort, which always happens when one confronts a distressing truth, but it should not create any permanent damage to mental acuity. I'm sure for those of you people who read my poetry and think me a poor speller, the words *lie*, *their*, *were*, and *grey* have a reason for being used that way. Read the poems again, and think with your spirit when you read them, and for those that think I can write only military prose and have no romantic inclinations, I offer this one that was recently written:

Lovers

Hand in hand, they stroll by the sea
Love unfurled only they can be

Tides and time are theirs to command
Only the pair and God can understand

Hidden by the night, betrayed by the moon
Two that walk the way that lovers do

Crashing waves bow to the beat of their heated hearts
Footprints away not to display what art

The ways of LOVE

In closing, let me remind you of something: Over 1,600 years ago, at the Council of NICEA, seventy-two clerics assembled the Bible as we know it, the inspired Word of God. The Bible gave us spiritual freedom but made us subject to Caesar; and in 1787 and 1789, fifty-five delegates came together in Philadelphia, Pennsylvania (remember the Church of Philadelphia)—also, I believe, inspired by God—and gave us the Constitution, our legal ability to exercise free will. They are both worth fighting for and obeying, I think. Read REVELATIONS 3:7 The Constitution is one of the things we have to hold on to.